Rachel Frank

Raw Energy Bar Invasion

Rachel Frank is a Board Certified Holistic Health Coach, PhD candidate, and Army Wife. Since childhood she has dreamed of writing books and helping others through her words and classes. She started her writing career with the *Healthy Tastes Great Vegan Cookbook* series and never looked back.

D1562852

BOOKS BY RACHEL FRANK

Healthy Tastes Great Vegan Cookbook: Volume 1 Breakfast

Healthy Tastes Great Vegan Cookbook: Volume 2 Bread

Stress the Silent Killer: Stress Management Techniques for Fighting Back

Raw Energy Bar Invasion
50 Fruit and Nut Bar Recipes

Rachel Frank, MS

ISBN: 0615808999
ISBN-13: 978-0615808994

http://www.happyhealthpublishing.com

DEDICATION

For my husband, if only you knew what you were getting into when you asked for healthy snacks that would fit in your ACU pocket...

CONTENTS

ACKNOWLEDGMENTS

I was inspired to explore vegan and raw cooking from my own health issues and those of my family. I have endometriosis and degenerative disk disease which are irritated by estrogen and inflammatory foods. This first sparked my interest in dairy free and healthy cooking. My parents and grandparents all have high cholesterol and high blood pressure. This lead to further exploration into egg free and healthy cooking.

My family has been amazing during this process. They have tasted every success and flop, cheered me on, and been a shoulder to lean on when I was exhausted from long days in the kitchen and at the computer.

I was inspired by many cookbook authors, TV cooking shows, and chefs. My favorites include Colleen Patrick-Goudreau, Chloe Coscarelli, The Vegan Zombie, and The Sweetest Vegan. Their books, recipes, videos, and passion for vegan cooking were inspiring and motivating.

A chin scratching to my crazy critters who kept me company all of those hours in front of the computer. Just so you know how crazy I am here they are: Mama, Twinkie, Onyx, Waffles, Princess, Critter, Grunt, Tessa, Barney, Bonnie, Squeaker, Itty Bitty, Angel, Brucey, Nugget, and Nibbler. Thanks for keeping my feet warm, purring me on, and adding your own crazy typos to my initial drafts. Anyone else scared at how that took just as much space as my human thank yous?!

PART 1
INTRODUCTION

MY STORY

My husband is a Drill Sergeant in the United States Army. During the day he barely has time to breathe let alone eat. One day he came to me asking for snacks to bring to work that were healthy, portable, delicious, and high in protein and fiber. So, like any wife would do I started buying prepackaged snacks like Larabars, Luna Bars, and 100 calorie snack packs of nuts and trail mixes.

At first this seemed like the sensible thing to do. I mean he was getting healthy whole foods and they fit all of his requirements. However, I soon realized this was getting expensive! Now don't get me wrong, I love spending money on healthy food. But this was spiraling out of control and I knew there had to be a better way.

I was already familiar with healthy eating and cooking with my background in holistic nutrition. I had even published a vegan cookbook and was working on another. So, the lightbulb went off! Make my own bars at home like I used to when my husband was deployed and write down all of my recipes.

WHY RAW FOODS ROCK

What is raw food?

Raw food is food that is uncooked and in its natural state. Food can be heated up to 117 F (48 C) and still be considered raw food. It can also be referred to as living or live food. Raw foods can include fruits, vegetables, herbs, nuts, seed, beans, grains, sea vegetables, oils, algae, spices, sweeteners, and super-foods.

Why is raw food so good for you?

Eating raw food is great for your body. When food is raw, the life force energy, enzymes, water, vitamins, minerals, and nutritional content of the food are readily available for the body in high concentrations. This means you get more nutritional value from the foods you eat! Now that is just a general rule. There are some foods where the nutritional value increases after it has been cooked or are easier to digest in their cooked state, but for the majority of raw foods this is not the case.

Health Benefits of Raw Foods:
- •Increased energy
- •Weight loss
- •Look younger
- •Clearer skin
- •Shinier hair
- •Stronger nails
- •Reduced cholesterol

- Reduced blood pressure
- Reduced aches & pains
- Reduced inflammation
- Improved overall health
- Improved mood

Nutrients in Fruits:

Apples - vitamin C, B-complex vitamins, beta-carotene, antioxidants, & potassium

Apricots - vitamin A, vitamin C, beta-carotene, iron, zinc, potassium, calcium , & manganese

Bananas - vitamin B-6, vitamin C, fiber, beta-carotene, copper, magnesium, & potassium

Blackberries - vitamin A, vitamin E, vitamin C, B-complex vitamins, fiber, potassium, & copper

Blueberries - B-complex vitamins, fiber, potassium, manganese, copper, iron, & zinc

Cherries - melatonin, potassium, zinc, iron, copper, beta-carotene, & manganese

Dates - vitamin A, beta-carotene, fiber, tannins, iron, potassium, calcium, copper, & B-complex

Goji Berries - vitamin A, vitamin C, calcium, selenium, & iron

Grapes/ Raisins - vitamin A, vitamin C, b-complex, potassium, copper, iron, resveratrol, & catechins

Kiwi - vitamin C, vitamin A, vitamin E, vitamin K, omega 3 fatty acids, potassium, & manganese

Lemons - vitamin C, vitamin A, B-complex, phyto-chemicals, calcium, iron, potassium, & copper

Limes - vitamin C, vitamin A, B-complex, phyto-chemicals, calcium, iron, potassium, & copper

Mango - vitamin A, vitamin C, vitamin E, beta-carotene, vitamin B-6, & copper

Mulberries - B-complex, anthocyanins, resveratrol, potassium, magnesium, & iron

Oranges - vitamin C, vitamin A, B-complex, fiber, phyto-chemicals, potassium, & calcium

Peaches - vitamin A, vitamin C, beta-carotene, lutein, zea-xanthin, potassium, flouride, & iron

Pears - vitamin C, vitamin A, beta-carotene, fiber, copper, iron, potassium, & magnesium

Pineapples - vitamin C, vitamin A, B-Complex, beta-carotene, copper, magnesium & potassium

Raspberries - vitamin C, vitamin A, vitamin E, B-complex, potassium, copper, iron, & manganese

Nutrients in Nuts & Seeds:
Almonds - vitamin E, B-complex, fiber, potassium, calcium, iron, zinc, & selenium

Cashews - monounsaturated fats, manganese, potassium, copper, iron, zinc, & zea-xanthin

Chia Seeds - omega 3 fatty acids, omega 6, fiber, & calcium

Coconut - lauric acid, cytokinins, copper, calcium, ison, potassium, manganese, magnesium, & zinc

Flaxseeds - oleic acid, omega 3 fatty acids, vitamin E, B-complex, calcium, potassium, & manganese

Hazelnuts - fiber, folate, vitamin E, B-complex, calcium, iron, copper, zinc, magnesium, & potassium

Peanuts - oleic acid, resveratrol, vitamin E, B-complex, calcium, potassium, copper, iron, & selenium

Pecans - oelic acid, ellagic acid, vitamin E, B-complex, beta-carotene, calcium, potassium, & iron

Pumpkin Seeds - oelic acid, tryptophan, glutamate, vitamin E, B-complex, & superoxide dismutase

Sunflower Seeds - linoleic acid, oelic acid, folic acid, calcium, niacin, selenium, iron, & manganese

Walnuts - omega 3 fatty acids, vitamin E, B-complex, manganese, copper, iron, calcium, & potassium

How much raw is right for me?

Each individual has a unique personality and this applies to their food personality as well. Some people thrive on a particular diet like raw or vegan, while others do not. The key is finding the balance point at which you feel great and are healthy.

For example, I eat a 90% vegan diet only consuming dairy in small amounts when I travel or attend family holiday gatherings and I cannot control what type of butter or milk the dishes were cooked with. About 50-75% of my vegan diet is raw. I feel fantastic with this type of eating plan, but it took me some trail and error to find this balance worked great for me. By switching to this diet, from a vegetarian diet, I have lowered my blood pressure, reduced inflammation in my spine, and eliminated my endometriosis pain!

While my husband is the complete opposite. Normally, he eats meat daily, eggs several times a week, has milk daily, and my vegan and raw foods serve as snacks or side dishes to his standard meals. Now, he is eating more vegan and raw foods after seeing how much they increase his energy for his workouts and how he feels less bloated and weighed down by the food he eats. His favorite raw vegan foods are my snack bars from this book, large salads, and smoothies.

You will need to try this trial and error process for yourself. It takes 4 weeks to change a habit, and for a lot of us the foods we eat are just that, habits. Try eating more raw food snacks in place of processed snacks for a month and examine the results of that experiment. I bet you will end up feeling more energized, have less pain/ inflammation, and will shed a couple of pounds. This is where change starts. So why not make it a tasty change!

FRUIT AND NUT BAR BASICS

Making fruit and nut bars is so simple to do at home. There are only a few ingredients, you can make them ahead of time, and they can be stored for several weeks or months! I hope you enjoy the recipes in this book and have fun experimenting with flavors and combinations of your own.

This cookbook has 50 amazing versions for you to try. There a couple of extra recipes in the book. First, there is a recipe for making raw vanilla "extract" which can be used in the recipes. **If you want to use traditional vanilla extract, only use 1/2 of what the recipe calls for.** Second, I have included my Raw Homemade Granola Recipe that is used in one of the bars. This granola is also wonderful for breakfast with fresh fruit or almond milk. Additionally, if you are a visual learner, I have included a link in the resources section to a video showing me making the bars with the basic directions provided below.

Basic Directions for All Bars:
1 - Place all of the ingredients into a food processor. Pulse several times to start breaking the larger pieces up.
2 - Process the mixture for 1-3 minutes until everything is broken down into tiny pieces and sticking together.
3 - Gather the fruit/ nut mixture into a ball and mash together with your hands.
4 - Divide the mixture into the number of bars you want to make.

5 - With damp hands flatten the mixture into a rectangle 3-4" tall rectangle, cover tightly with the plastic wrap, and apply a lot of pressure. Repeat with all remaining mixture sections.
6 - Allow the mixture to chill flat in the refrigerator for one hour to overnight.
7 - Label and enjoy!

Storage:
Store the bars wrapped individually in plastic wrap. Label the bars for reference. They can be stored for up to 2 weeks in the refrigerator and 2 months in the freezer.

Drying Fruit at Home:
1 - Halve, quarter, slice, or dice the fruit toto the desired shape and thickness.
2 - Lay the fruit flat on a dehydrator tray.
3 - Bake 115F for 10-18 hours or until fruit is dried to your liking.
* Time will vary based on fruit and thickness of the pieces.

Nutritional Information (estimates based on an average bar):
Average Bar Size - 45g
Calories - 175g
Fat Calories - 80g
Total Fat - 8g
Cholesterol - 0g
Sodium - <1g
Potassium - 400mg
Carbohydrates - 30g
Fiber - 4g
Sugar - 23g
Fiber - 5g

RACHEL FRANK

PART 2
RECIPES

BREAKFAST FLAVORS

Ultimate Power Punch

3/4 Cup Medjool Dates, Pitted
3/4 Cup Almonds
2 Tb Goji Berries
1 tsp Chia Seeds
1 Tb Flaxseeds
3/4 tsp Vanilla
Pinch of Sea Salt

Directions:

1 - Place all of the ingredients into a food processor. Pulse several times to start breaking the larger pieces up.

2 - Process the mixture for 1-3 minutes until everything is broken down into tiny pieces and sticking together.

3 - Gather the fruit/ nut mixture into a ball and mash together with your hands.

4 - Divide the mixture into the number of bars you want to make.

5 - With damp hands flatten the mixture into a rectangle 3-4" tall rectangle, cover tightly with the plastic wrap, and apply a lot of pressure. Repeat with all remaining mixture sections.

6 - Allow the mixture to chill flat in the refrigerator for one hour to overnight.

7 - Label and enjoy!

Grandma's Granola

1/2 Cup Raw Homemade Granola
1/2 Cup Medjool Dates, Pitted

Directions:
1 - Place all of the ingredients into a food processor. Pulse several times to start breaking the larger pieces up.
2 - Process the mixture for 1-3 minutes until everything is broken down into tiny pieces and sticking together.
3 - Gather the fruit/ nut mixture into a ball and mash together with your hands.
4 - Divide the mixture into the number of bars you want to make.
5 - With damp hands flatten the mixture into a rectangle 3-4" tall rectangle, cover tightly with the plastic wrap, and apply a lot of pressure. Repeat with all remaining mixture sections.
6 - Allow the mixture to chill flat in the refrigerator for one hour to overnight.
7 - Label and enjoy!

Breakfast Nut

1/2 Cup Sunflower Seeds
1/2 Cup Medjool Dates, Pitted
2 tsp Honey
Pinch of Sea Salt
1/2 tsp Vanilla

Directions:

1 - Place all of the ingredients into a food processor. Pulse several times to start breaking the larger pieces up.

2 - Process the mixture for 1-3 minutes until everything is broken down into tiny pieces and sticking together.

3 - Gather the fruit/ nut mixture into a ball and mash together with your hands.

4 - Divide the mixture into the number of bars you want to make.

5 - With damp hands flatten the mixture into a rectangle 3-4" tall rectangle, cover tightly with the plastic wrap, and apply a lot of pressure. Repeat with all remaining mixture sections.

6 - Allow the mixture to chill flat in the refrigerator for one hour to overnight.

7 - Label and enjoy!

House Blend

1/2 Cup Cashews
1 Cup Medjool Dates, Pitted
Pinch of Sea Salt
1/2 tsp Vanilla
1/2 Cup Caffeine Free Tea
* Soak the cashews in the tea for at least 1 hour to overnight , drain, discard tea, then mix as normal.

Directions:
1 - Place all of the ingredients into a food processor. Pulse several times to start breaking the larger pieces up.
2 - Process the mixture for 1-3 minutes until everything is broken down into tiny pieces and sticking together.
3 - Gather the fruit/ nut mixture into a ball and mash together with your hands.
4 - Divide the mixture into the number of bars you want to make.
5 - With damp hands flatten the mixture into a rectangle 3-4" tall rectangle, cover tightly with the plastic wrap, and apply a lot of pressure. Repeat with all remaining mixture sections.
6 - Allow the mixture to chill flat in the refrigerator for one hour to overnight.
7 - Label and enjoy!

Mocha Mambo

1/2 Cup Cashews
1/2 Cup Hazelnuts
1 Cup Medjool Dates, Pitted
2 Tb Cocoa Powder
2 Tb Dark Chocolate Chips
Pinch of Sea Salt
1/2 tsp Vanilla
1/2 Cup Caffeine Free Tea
* Soak the cashews in the tea for at least 1 hour to overnight , drain, discard tea, then mix as normal.

Directions:

1 - Place all of the ingredients into a food processor. Pulse several times to start breaking the larger pieces up.
2 - Process the mixture for 1-3 minutes until everything is broken down into tiny pieces and sticking together.
3 - Gather the fruit/ nut mixture into a ball and mash together with your hands.
4 - Divide the mixture into the number of bars you want to make.
5 - With damp hands flatten the mixture into a rectangle 3-4" tall rectangle, cover tightly with the plastic wrap, and apply a lot of pressure. Repeat with all remaining mixture sections.
6 - Allow the mixture to chill flat in the refrigerator for one hour to overnight.
7 - Label and enjoy!

SMOOTHIE FLAVORS

Strawberry Banana

1/2 Cup Almonds
1/2 Cup Cashews
1 Cup Medjool Dates, Pitted
1/2 Cup Dried Strawberries
1/2 Cup Dried Bananas
Pinch of Sea Salt
1/2 tsp Vanilla

Directions:
1 - Place all of the ingredients into a food processor. Pulse several times to start breaking the larger pieces up.
2 - Process the mixture for 1-3 minutes until everything is broken down into tiny pieces and sticking together.
3 - Gather the fruit/ nut mixture into a ball and mash together with your hands.
4 - Divide the mixture into the number of bars you want to make.
5 - With damp hands flatten the mixture into a rectangle 3-4" tall rectangle, cover tightly with the plastic wrap, and apply a lot of pressure. Repeat with all remaining mixture sections.
6 - Allow the mixture to chill flat in the refrigerator for one hour to overnight.
7 - Label and enjoy!

Strawberry Spritzer

1/2 Cup Almonds
1/2 Cup Cashews
1 Cup Medjool Dates, Pitted
1/4 Cup Dried Strawberries
1/2 Cup Dried Pineapple
Pinch of Sea Salt
1/2 tsp Vanilla

Directions:
1 - Place all of the ingredients into a food processor. Pulse several times to start breaking the larger pieces up.
2 - Process the mixture for 1-3 minutes until everything is broken down into tiny pieces and sticking together.
3 - Gather the fruit/ nut mixture into a ball and mash together with your hands.
4 - Divide the mixture into the number of bars you want to make.
5 - With damp hands flatten the mixture into a rectangle 3-4" tall rectangle, cover tightly with the plastic wrap, and apply a lot of pressure. Repeat with all remaining mixture sections.
6 - Allow the mixture to chill flat in the refrigerator for one hour to overnight.
7 - Label and enjoy!

Razz Tastic

1/2 Cup Almonds
1/2 Cup Cashews
1 Cup Medjool Dates, Pitted
1/4 Cup Dried Strawberries
1/4 Cup Dried Bananas
1/4 Cup Dried Raspberries
Pinch of Sea Salt
1/2 tsp Vanilla

Directions:
1 - Place all of the ingredients into a food processor. Pulse several times to start breaking the larger pieces up.
2 - Process the mixture for 1-3 minutes until everything is broken down into tiny pieces and sticking together.
3 - Gather the fruit/ nut mixture into a ball and mash together with your hands.
4 - Divide the mixture into the number of bars you want to make.
5 - With damp hands flatten the mixture into a rectangle 3-4" tall rectangle, cover tightly with the plastic wrap, and apply a lot of pressure. Repeat with all remaining mixture sections.
6 - Allow the mixture to chill flat in the refrigerator for one hour to overnight.
7 - Label and enjoy!

Blue Balls

1/2 Cup Almonds
1/2 Cup Cashews
1 Cup Medjool Dates, Pitted
1/4 Cup Dried Strawberries
1/4 Cup Dried Bananas
1/4 Cup Dried Blueberries
Pinch of Sea Salt
1/2 tsp Vanilla

Directions:

1 - Place all of the ingredients into a food processor. Pulse several times to start breaking the larger pieces up.

2 - Process the mixture for 1-3 minutes until everything is broken down into tiny pieces and sticking together.

3 - Gather the fruit/ nut mixture into a ball and mash together with your hands.

4 - Divide the mixture into the number of bars you want to make.

5 - With damp hands flatten the mixture into a rectangle 3-4" tall rectangle, cover tightly with the plastic wrap, and apply a lot of pressure. Repeat with all remaining mixture sections.

6 - Allow the mixture to chill flat in the refrigerator for one hour to overnight.

7 - Label and enjoy!

Black Cherry

1/2 Cup Almonds
1/2 Cup Cashews
1 Cup Medjool Dates, Pitted
1/2 Cup Dried Cherries
1/4 Cup Dried Black Berries
Pinch of Sea Salt
1/2 tsp Vanilla

Directions:
1 - Place all of the ingredients into a food processor. Pulse several times to start breaking the larger pieces up.
2 - Process the mixture for 1-3 minutes until everything is broken down into tiny pieces and sticking together.
3 - Gather the fruit/ nut mixture into a ball and mash together with your hands.
4 - Divide the mixture into the number of bars you want to make.
5 - With damp hands flatten the mixture into a rectangle 3-4" tall rectangle, cover tightly with the plastic wrap, and apply a lot of pressure. Repeat with all remaining mixture sections.
6 - Allow the mixture to chill flat in the refrigerator for one hour to overnight.
7 - Label and enjoy!

Hawaiian Surf

1/2 Cup Almonds
1/2 Cup Cashews
1 Cup Medjool Dates, Pitted
1/4 Cup Dried Strawberries
1/4 Cup Dried Peaches
1/4 Cup Dried Mango
Pinch of Sea Salt
1/2 tsp Vanilla

Directions:

1 - Place all of the ingredients into a food processor. Pulse several times to start breaking the larger pieces up.

2 - Process the mixture for 1-3 minutes until everything is broken down into tiny pieces and sticking together.

3 - Gather the fruit/ nut mixture into a ball and mash together with your hands.

4 - Divide the mixture into the number of bars you want to make.

5 - With damp hands flatten the mixture into a rectangle 3-4" tall rectangle, cover tightly with the plastic wrap, and apply a lot of pressure. Repeat with all remaining mixture sections.

6 - Allow the mixture to chill flat in the refrigerator for one hour to overnight.

7 - Label and enjoy!

Strawberry Whirl

1/2 Cup Almonds
1/2 Cup Cashews
1 Cup Medjool Dates, Pitted
1/4 Cup Dried Strawberries
1/4 Cup Dried Bananas
1/4 Cup Dried Apples
Pinch of Sea Salt
1/2 tsp Vanilla

Directions:

1 - Place all of the ingredients into a food processor. Pulse several times to start breaking the larger pieces up.

2 - Process the mixture for 1-3 minutes until everything is broken down into tiny pieces and sticking together.

3 - Gather the fruit/ nut mixture into a ball and mash together with your hands.

4 - Divide the mixture into the number of bars you want to make.

5 - With damp hands flatten the mixture into a rectangle 3-4" tall rectangle, cover tightly with the plastic wrap, and apply a lot of pressure. Repeat with all remaining mixture sections.

6 - Allow the mixture to chill flat in the refrigerator for one hour to overnight.

7 - Label and enjoy!

Strawberry Kiwi

1/2 Cup Almonds
1/2 Cup Cashews
1 Cup Medjool Dates, Pitted
1/2 Cup Dried Strawberries
1/2 Cup Dried Kiwi
Pinch of Sea Salt
1/2 tsp Vanilla

Directions:
1 - Place all of the ingredients into a food processor. Pulse several times to start breaking the larger pieces up.
2 - Process the mixture for 1-3 minutes until everything is broken down into tiny pieces and sticking together.
3 - Gather the fruit/ nut mixture into a ball and mash together with your hands.
4 - Divide the mixture into the number of bars you want to make.
5 - With damp hands flatten the mixture into a rectangle 3-4" tall rectangle, cover tightly with the plastic wrap, and apply a lot of pressure. Repeat with all remaining mixture sections.
6 - Allow the mixture to chill flat in the refrigerator for one hour to overnight.
7 - Label and enjoy!

5 a Day

1/2 Cup Almonds
1/2 Cup Cashews
1 Cup Medjool Dates, Pitted
1/8 Cup Dried Strawberries
1/8 Cup Dried Blueberry
1/4 Cup Dried Mango
1/4 Cup Dried Peaches
1/4 Cup Dried Bananas
Pinch of Sea Salt
1/2 tsp Vanilla

Directions:

1 - Place all of the ingredients into a food processor. Pulse several times to start breaking the larger pieces up.

2 - Process the mixture for 1-3 minutes until everything is broken down into tiny pieces and sticking together.

3 - Gather the fruit/ nut mixture into a ball and mash together with your hands.

4 - Divide the mixture into the number of bars you want to make.

5 - With damp hands flatten the mixture into a rectangle 3-4" tall rectangle, cover tightly with the plastic wrap, and apply a lot of pressure. Repeat with all remaining mixture sections.

6 - Allow the mixture to chill flat in the refrigerator for one hour to overnight.

7 - Label and enjoy!

Peach Paradise

1/2 Cup Almonds
1/2 Cup Cashews
1 Cup Medjool Dates, Pitted
1/4 Cup Dried Peaches
1/4 Cup Dried Mango
Pinch of Sea Salt
1/2 tsp VanillaPeach Mango

Directions:
1 - Place all of the ingredients into a food processor. Pulse several times to start breaking the larger pieces up.
2 - Process the mixture for 1-3 minutes until everything is broken down into tiny pieces and sticking together.
3 - Gather the fruit/ nut mixture into a ball and mash together with your hands.
4 - Divide the mixture into the number of bars you want to make.
5 - With damp hands flatten the mixture into a rectangle 3-4" tall rectangle, cover tightly with the plastic wrap, and apply a lot of pressure. Repeat with all remaining mixture sections.
6 - Allow the mixture to chill flat in the refrigerator for one hour to overnight.
7 - Label and enjoy!

BREAD & MUFFIN FLAVORS

PB & J

1 Cup Peanuts
1 Cup Medjool Dates, Pitted
1 Cup Dried Cherries
Pinch of Sea Salt
1/2 tsp Vanilla

Directions:

1 - Place all of the ingredients into a food processor. Pulse several times to start breaking the larger pieces up.

2 - Process the mixture for 1-3 minutes until everything is broken down into tiny pieces and sticking together.

3 - Gather the fruit/ nut mixture into a ball and mash together with your hands.

4 - Divide the mixture into the number of bars you want to make.

5 - With damp hands flatten the mixture into a rectangle 3-4" tall rectangle, cover tightly with the plastic wrap, and apply a lot of pressure. Repeat with all remaining mixture sections.

6 - Allow the mixture to chill flat in the refrigerator for one hour to overnight.

7 - Label and enjoy!

Banana Bread

1 Cup Almonds
1 Cup Medjool Dates, Pitted
1 Cup Dried Bananas
Pinch of Sea Salt
1/2 tsp Vanilla

Directions:
1 - Place all of the ingredients into a food processor. Pulse several times to start breaking the larger pieces up.
2 - Process the mixture for 1-3 minutes until everything is broken down into tiny pieces and sticking together.
3 - Gather the fruit/ nut mixture into a ball and mash together with your hands.
4 - Divide the mixture into the number of bars you want to make.
5 - With damp hands flatten the mixture into a rectangle 3-4" tall rectangle, cover tightly with the plastic wrap, and apply a lot of pressure. Repeat with all remaining mixture sections.
6 - Allow the mixture to chill flat in the refrigerator for one hour to overnight.
7 - Label and enjoy!

Blueberry Muffin

1 Cup Cashews
1 Cup Medjool Dates, Pitted
1 Cup Dried Blueberries
Pinch of Sea Salt
1/2 tsp Vanilla

Directions:
1 - Place all of the ingredients into a food processor. Pulse several times to start breaking the larger pieces up.
2 - Process the mixture for 1-3 minutes until everything is broken down into tiny pieces and sticking together.
3 - Gather the fruit/ nut mixture into a ball and mash together with your hands.
4 - Divide the mixture into the number of bars you want to make.
5 - With damp hands flatten the mixture into a rectangle 3-4" tall rectangle, cover tightly with the plastic wrap, and apply a lot of pressure. Repeat with all remaining mixture sections.
6 - Allow the mixture to chill flat in the refrigerator for one hour to overnight.
7 - Label and enjoy!

Cinnamon Swirl

1/2 Cup Cashews
1 Cup Medjool Dates, Pitted
Pinch of Sea Salt
Pinch Cinnamon
2 Tb Rasins

Directions:

1 - Place all of the ingredients into a food processor. Pulse several times to start breaking the larger pieces up.

2 - Process the mixture for 1-3 minutes until everything is broken down into tiny pieces and sticking together.

3 - Gather the fruit/ nut mixture into a ball and mash together with your hands.

4 - Divide the mixture into the number of bars you want to make.

5 - With damp hands flatten the mixture into a rectangle 3-4" tall rectangle, cover tightly with the plastic wrap, and apply a lot of pressure. Repeat with all remaining mixture sections.

6 - Allow the mixture to chill flat in the refrigerator for one hour to overnight.

7 - Label and enjoy!

COOKIE FLAVORS

Cashew Cookie

1/2 Cup Cashews
1 Cup Medjool Dates, Pitted
Pinch of Sea Salt
1/2 tsp Vanilla

Directions:
1 - Place all of the ingredients into a food processor. Pulse several times to start breaking the larger pieces up.
2 - Process the mixture for 1-3 minutes until everything is broken down into tiny pieces and sticking together.
3 - Gather the fruit/ nut mixture into a ball and mash together with your hands.
4 - Divide the mixture into the number of bars you want to make.
5 - With damp hands flatten the mixture into a rectangle 3-4" tall rectangle, cover tightly with the plastic wrap, and apply a lot of pressure. Repeat with all remaining mixture sections.
6 - Allow the mixture to chill flat in the refrigerator for one hour to overnight.
7 - Label and enjoy!

Chocolate Chip Cookie

1/2 Cup Cashews
1 Cup Medjool Dates, Pitted
Pinch of Sea Salt
1/2 tsp Vanilla
1 Tb Chocolate Chips/ Cocoa Nibs

Directions:

1 - Place all of the ingredients into a food processor. Pulse several times to start breaking the larger pieces up.

2 - Process the mixture for 1-3 minutes until everything is broken down into tiny pieces and sticking together.

3 - Gather the fruit/ nut mixture into a ball and mash together with your hands.

4 - Divide the mixture into the number of bars you want to make.

5 - With damp hands flatten the mixture into a rectangle 3-4" tall rectangle, cover tightly with the plastic wrap, and apply a lot of pressure. Repeat with all remaining mixture sections.

6 - Allow the mixture to chill flat in the refrigerator for one hour to overnight.

7 - Label and enjoy!

Chocolate Chip Peanut Butter Cookie

1/2 Cup Peanuts
1 Cup Medjool Dates, Pitted
Pinch of Sea Salt
1/2 tsp Vanilla
2 Tb Chocolate Chips

Directions:
1 - Place all of the ingredients into a food processor. Pulse several times to start breaking the larger pieces up.
2 - Process the mixture for 1-3 minutes until everything is broken down into tiny pieces and sticking together.
3 - Gather the fruit/ nut mixture into a ball and mash together with your hands.
4 - Divide the mixture into the number of bars you want to make.
5 - With damp hands flatten the mixture into a rectangle 3-4" tall rectangle, cover tightly with the plastic wrap, and apply a lot of pressure. Repeat with all remaining mixture sections.
6 - Allow the mixture to chill flat in the refrigerator for one hour to overnight.
7 - Label and enjoy!

Chocolate Buckwheat Cookie

3/4 Cup Rasins
6 Tb Dehydrated Buckwheat
3/4 Cup Almonds
1/2 tsp Vanilla
3 Tb Cocoa Powder
1 Tb Chocolate Chips
Pinch of Sea Salt

Directions:
1 - Place all of the ingredients into a food processor. Pulse several times to start breaking the larger pieces up.
2 - Process the mixture for 1-3 minutes until everything is broken down into tiny pieces and sticking together.
3 - Gather the fruit/ nut mixture into a ball and mash together with your hands.
4 - Divide the mixture into the number of bars you want to make.
5 - With damp hands flatten the mixture into a rectangle 3-4" tall rectangle, cover tightly with the plastic wrap, and apply a lot of pressure. Repeat with all remaining mixture sections.
6 - Allow the mixture to chill flat in the refrigerator for one hour to overnight.
7 - Label and enjoy!

Chocolate Macaroon

1/2 Cup Cashews
1/2 Cup Medjool Dates, Pitted
2 Tb Cocoa Powder
1/4 Cup Shredded Coconut
Pinch of Sea Salt
1/2 tsp Vanilla

Directions:
1 - Place all of the ingredients into a food processor. Pulse several times to start breaking the larger pieces up.
2 - Process the mixture for 1-3 minutes until everything is broken down into tiny pieces and sticking together.
3 - Gather the fruit/ nut mixture into a ball and mash together with your hands.
4 - Divide the mixture into the number of bars you want to make.
5 - With damp hands flatten the mixture into a rectangle 3-4" tall rectangle, cover tightly with the plastic wrap, and apply a lot of pressure. Repeat with all remaining mixture sections.
6 - Allow the mixture to chill flat in the refrigerator for one hour to overnight.
7 - Label and enjoy!

Thin Mints

1/2 Cup Cashews
1 Cup Medjool Dates, Pitted
Pinch of Sea Salt
1/8 tsp Peppermint
2 Tb Cocoa Powder
1 tsp Cocoa Nibs (optional)

Directions:
1 - Place all of the ingredients into a food processor. Pulse several times to start breaking the larger pieces up.
2 - Process the mixture for 1-3 minutes until everything is broken down into tiny pieces and sticking together.
3 - Gather the fruit/ nut mixture into a ball and mash together with your hands.
4 - Divide the mixture into the number of bars you want to make.
5 - With damp hands flatten the mixture into a rectangle 3-4" tall rectangle, cover tightly with the plastic wrap, and apply a lot of pressure. Repeat with all remaining mixture sections.
6 - Allow the mixture to chill flat in the refrigerator for one hour to overnight.
7 - Label and enjoy!

Almond Joy

1/2 Cup Almonds
1/2 Cup Medjool Dates, Pitted
2 Tb Cocoa Powder
1/4 Cup Shredded Coconut
1 Tb Coconut Oil
1/4 Cup Dark Chocolate Chips
Pinch of Sea Salt
1/2 tsp Vanilla

Directions:

1 - Place all of the ingredients into a food processor. Pulse several times to start breaking the larger pieces up.

2 - Process the mixture for 1-3 minutes until everything is broken down into tiny pieces and sticking together.

3 - Gather the fruit/ nut mixture into a ball and mash together with your hands.

4 - Divide the mixture into the number of bars you want to make.

5 - With damp hands flatten the mixture into a rectangle 3-4" tall rectangle, cover tightly with the plastic wrap, and apply a lot of pressure. Repeat with all remaining mixture sections.

6 - Allow the mixture to chill flat in the refrigerator for one hour to overnight.

7 - Label and enjoy!

Snickerdoodles

1/2 Cup Cashews
1 Cup Medjool Dates, Pitted
Pinch of Sea Salt
1/2 tsp Vanilla
Cinnamon Sugar

Directions:
1 - Place all of the ingredients into a food processor. Pulse several times to start breaking the larger pieces up.
2 - Process the mixture for 1-3 minutes until everything is broken down into tiny pieces and sticking together.
3 - Gather the fruit/ nut mixture into a ball and mash together with your hands.
4 - Divide the mixture into the number of bars you want to make.
5 - With damp hands flatten the mixture into a rectangle 3-4" tall rectangle, cover tightly with the plastic wrap, and apply a lot of pressure. Repeat with all remaining mixture sections.
6 - Allow the mixture to chill flat in the refrigerator for one hour to overnight.
7 - Label and enjoy!

Samoas Cookie Bar

1 Cup Medjool Dates, Pitted
4 Tb Unsweetened Shredded Coconut
1/2 tsp Vanilla
Pinch of Sea Salt
1-2 Tb Chocolate Chips

Directions:
1 - Place all of the ingredients into a food processor. Pulse several times to start breaking the larger pieces up.
2 - Process the mixture for 1-3 minutes until everything is broken down into tiny pieces and sticking together.
3 - Gather the fruit/ nut mixture into a ball and mash together with your hands.
4 - Divide the mixture into the number of bars you want to make.
5 - With damp hands flatten the mixture into a rectangle 3-4" tall rectangle, cover tightly with the plastic wrap, and apply a lot of pressure. Repeat with all remaining mixture sections.
6 - Allow the mixture to chill flat in the refrigerator for one hour to overnight.
7 - Label and enjoy!

Peanut Butter Cookie

1/2 Cup Peanuts
1 Cup Medjool Dates, Pitted
Pinch of Sea Salt
1/2 tsp Vanilla

Directions:
1 - Place all of the ingredients into a food processor. Pulse several times to start breaking the larger pieces up.
2 - Process the mixture for 1-3 minutes until everything is broken down into tiny pieces and sticking together.
3 - Gather the fruit/ nut mixture into a ball and mash together with your hands.
4 - Divide the mixture into the number of bars you want to make.
5 - With damp hands flatten the mixture into a rectangle 3-4" tall rectangle, cover tightly with the plastic wrap, and apply a lot of pressure. Repeat with all remaining mixture sections.
6 - Allow the mixture to chill flat in the refrigerator for one hour to overnight.
7 - Label and enjoy!

Gingerbread

1 Cup Medjool Dates, Pitted
1/4 Cup Almonds
1/4 tsp Ground Ginger
1/4 tsp Cinnamon
1/8 tsp Nutmeg
Pinch Cloves
1/2 tsp Vanilla
Pinch of Sea Salt

Directions:
1 - Place all of the ingredients into a food processor. Pulse several times to start breaking the larger pieces up.
2 - Process the mixture for 1-3 minutes until everything is broken down into tiny pieces and sticking together.
3 - Gather the fruit/ nut mixture into a ball and mash together with your hands.
4 - Divide the mixture into the number of bars you want to make.
5 - With damp hands flatten the mixture into a rectangle 3-4" tall rectangle, cover tightly with the plastic wrap, and apply a lot of pressure. Repeat with all remaining mixture sections.
6 - Allow the mixture to chill flat in the refrigerator for one hour to overnight.
7 - Label and enjoy!

Apricot Delight

1/2 Cup Almonds
1/4 Cup Walnuts
1 Cup Medjool Dates, Pitted
1/3 Cup Shredded Coconut
Pinch of Sea Salt
1/2 tsp Vanilla

Directions:

1 - Place all of the ingredients into a food processor. Pulse several times to start breaking the larger pieces up.

2 - Process the mixture for 1-3 minutes until everything is broken down into tiny pieces and sticking together.

3 - Gather the fruit/ nut mixture into a ball and mash together with your hands.

4 - Divide the mixture into the number of bars you want to make.

5 - With damp hands flatten the mixture into a rectangle 3-4" tall rectangle, cover tightly with the plastic wrap, and apply a lot of pressure. Repeat with all remaining mixture sections.

6 - Allow the mixture to chill flat in the refrigerator for one hour to overnight.

7 - Label and enjoy!

Lemon Bar

1/2 Cup Almonds
1/2 Cup Cashews
1 Cup Medjool Dates, Pitted
Zest & Juice 1 Lime
Pinch of Sea Salt
1/2 tsp Vanilla

Directions:

1 - Place all of the ingredients into a food processor. Pulse several times to start breaking the larger pieces up.

2 - Process the mixture for 1-3 minutes until everything is broken down into tiny pieces and sticking together.

3 - Gather the fruit/ nut mixture into a ball and mash together with your hands.

4 - Divide the mixture into the number of bars you want to make.

5 - With damp hands flatten the mixture into a rectangle 3-4" tall rectangle, cover tightly with the plastic wrap, and apply a lot of pressure. Repeat with all remaining mixture sections.

6 - Allow the mixture to chill flat in the refrigerator for one hour to overnight.

7 - Label and enjoy!

DESSERT FLAVORS

Brownie Bites

3/4 Cup Walnuts
1 Cup Medjool Dates, Pitted
1/2 tsp Vanilla
3 Tb Cocoa Powder
1 Tb Chocolate Chips
Pinch of Sea Salt

Directions:
1 - Place all of the ingredients into a food processor. Pulse several times to start breaking the larger pieces up.
2 - Process the mixture for 1-3 minutes until everything is broken down into tiny pieces and sticking together.
3 - Gather the fruit/ nut mixture into a ball and mash together with your hands.
4 - Divide the mixture into the number of bars you want to make.
5 - With damp hands flatten the mixture into a rectangle 3-4" tall rectangle, cover tightly with the plastic wrap, and apply a lot of pressure. Repeat with all remaining mixture sections.
6 - Allow the mixture to chill flat in the refrigerator for one hour to overnight.
7 - Label and enjoy!

Nutella

1/2 Cup Almonds
1/2 Cup Hazelnuts
1 Cup Medjool Dates, Pitted
2 Tb Cocoa Powder
2 Tb Dark Chocolate Chips
Pinch of Sea Salt
1/2 tsp Vanilla

Directions:
1 - Place all of the ingredients into a food processor. Pulse several times to start breaking the larger pieces up.
2 - Process the mixture for 1-3 minutes until everything is broken down into tiny pieces and sticking together.
3 - Gather the fruit/ nut mixture into a ball and mash together with your hands.
4 - Divide the mixture into the number of bars you want to make.
5 - With damp hands flatten the mixture into a rectangle 3-4" tall rectangle, cover tightly with the plastic wrap, and apply a lot of pressure. Repeat with all remaining mixture sections.
6 - Allow the mixture to chill flat in the refrigerator for one hour to overnight.
7 - Label and enjoy!

Bananas Foster

1/2 Cup Almonds
1/4 Cup Walnuts
1/4 Cup Pecans
1 Cup Medjool Dates, Pitted
3/4 Cup Dried Bananas
1 Tb Honey
1 tsp Cinnamon
Pinch of Sea Salt
1/2 tsp Vanilla

Directions:
1 - Place all of the ingredients into a food processor. Pulse several times to start breaking the larger pieces up.
2 - Process the mixture for 1-3 minutes until everything is broken down into tiny pieces and sticking together.
3 - Gather the fruit/ nut mixture into a ball and mash together with your hands.
4 - Divide the mixture into the number of bars you want to make.
5 - With damp hands flatten the mixture into a rectangle 3-4" tall rectangle, cover tightly with the plastic wrap, and apply a lot of pressure. Repeat with all remaining mixture sections.
6 - Allow the mixture to chill flat in the refrigerator for one hour to overnight.
7 - Label and enjoy!

Carrot Cake

1/2 Cup Almonds
1/2 Cup Walnuts
1 Cup Medjool Dates, Pitted
1/2 Cup Shredded Carrots
1/4 Cup Dried Pineapple
1/4 Cup Shredded Coconut
1 tsp Cinnamon
Pinch of Sea Salt

Directions:

1 - Place all of the ingredients into a food processor. Pulse several times to start breaking the larger pieces up.

2 - Process the mixture for 1-3 minutes until everything is broken down into tiny pieces and sticking together.

3 - Gather the fruit/ nut mixture into a ball and mash together with your hands.

4 - Divide the mixture into the number of bars you want to make.

5 - With damp hands flatten the mixture into a rectangle 3-4" tall rectangle, cover tightly with the plastic wrap, and apply a lot of pressure. Repeat with all remaining mixture sections.

6 - Allow the mixture to chill flat in the refrigerator for one hour to overnight.

7 - Label and enjoy!

Pineapple Pound Cake

1/2 Cup Almonds
1/2 Cup Sunflower Seeds
1 Cup Medjool Dates, Pitted
3/4 Cup Dried Pineapple
Pinch of Sea Salt
1/2 tsp Vanilla

Directions:
1 - Place all of the ingredients into a food processor. Pulse several times to start breaking the larger pieces up.
2 - Process the mixture for 1-3 minutes until everything is broken down into tiny pieces and sticking together.
3 - Gather the fruit/ nut mixture into a ball and mash together with your hands.
4 - Divide the mixture into the number of bars you want to make.
5 - With damp hands flatten the mixture into a rectangle 3-4" tall rectangle, cover tightly with the plastic wrap, and apply a lot of pressure. Repeat with all remaining mixture sections.
6 - Allow the mixture to chill flat in the refrigerator for one hour to overnight.
7 - Label and enjoy!

Apple Turnover

1/2 Cup Walntus
1/2 Cup Pecans
1 Cup Medjool Dates, Pitted
3/4 Cup Dried Apples
2 Tb Honey
1 tsp Cinnamon
Pinch of Sea Salt
1/2 tsp Vanilla

Directions:

1 - Place all of the ingredients into a food processor. Pulse several times to start breaking the larger pieces up.

2 - Process the mixture for 1-3 minutes until everything is broken down into tiny pieces and sticking together.

3 - Gather the fruit/ nut mixture into a ball and mash together with your hands.

4 - Divide the mixture into the number of bars you want to make.

5 - With damp hands flatten the mixture into a rectangle 3-4" tall rectangle, cover tightly with the plastic wrap, and apply a lot of pressure. Repeat with all remaining mixture sections.

6 - Allow the mixture to chill flat in the refrigerator for one hour to overnight.

7 - Label and enjoy!

Fruit Tart

1/2 Cup Almonds
1/2 Cup Cashews
1 Cup Medjool Dates, Pitted
1/2 Cup Dried Pineapple
1/2 Cup Shredded Coconut
Zest & Juice of 1 Small Orange
1 tsp Coconut Oil
Pinch of Sea Salt
1/2 tsp Vanilla

Directions:
1 - Place all of the ingredients into a food processor. Pulse several times to start breaking the larger pieces up.
2 - Process the mixture for 1-3 minutes until everything is broken down into tiny pieces and sticking together.
3 - Gather the fruit/ nut mixture into a ball and mash together with your hands.
4 - Divide the mixture into the number of bars you want to make.
5 - With damp hands flatten the mixture into a rectangle 3-4" tall rectangle, cover tightly with the plastic wrap, and apply a lot of pressure. Repeat with all remaining mixture sections.
6 - Allow the mixture to chill flat in the refrigerator for one hour to overnight.
7 - Label and enjoy!

Cinnamon Apple Crisp

1/2 Cup Peanuts
1/2 Cup Sunflower Seeds
1 Cup Medjool Dates, Pitted
1/2 Cup Dried Apples
1/4 tsp Cinnamon
Pinch of Sea Salt
1/2 tsp Vanilla

Directions:
1 - Place all of the ingredients into a food processor. Pulse several times to start breaking the larger pieces up.
2 - Process the mixture for 1-3 minutes until everything is broken down into tiny pieces and sticking together.
3 - Gather the fruit/ nut mixture into a ball and mash together with your hands.
4 - Divide the mixture into the number of bars you want to make.
5 - With damp hands flatten the mixture into a rectangle 3-4" tall rectangle, cover tightly with the plastic wrap, and apply a lot of pressure. Repeat with all remaining mixture sections.
6 - Allow the mixture to chill flat in the refrigerator for one hour to overnight.
7 - Label and enjoy!

Chocolate Covered Cherry

1/2 Cup Almonds
1/2 Cup Cashews
1 Cup Medjool Dates, Pitted
3/4 Cup Dried Cherries
1/4 Cup Chocolate Chips
Pinch of Sea Salt
1/2 tsp Vanilla

Directions:

1 - Place all of the ingredients into a food processor. Pulse several times to start breaking the larger pieces up.

2 - Process the mixture for 1-3 minutes until everything is broken down into tiny pieces and sticking together.

3 - Gather the fruit/ nut mixture into a ball and mash together with your hands.

4 - Divide the mixture into the number of bars you want to make.

5 - With damp hands flatten the mixture into a rectangle 3-4" tall rectangle, cover tightly with the plastic wrap, and apply a lot of pressure. Repeat with all remaining mixture sections.

6 - Allow the mixture to chill flat in the refrigerator for one hour to overnight.

7 - Label and enjoy!

Peach Cobbler

1/2 Cup Almonds
1/2 Cup Cashews
1 Cup Medjool Dates, Pitted
1 Cup Dried Peaches
Pinch of Sea Salt
1/2 tsp Vanilla

Directions:
1 - Place all of the ingredients into a food processor. Pulse several times to start breaking the larger pieces up.
2 - Process the mixture for 1-3 minutes until everything is broken down into tiny pieces and sticking together.
3 - Gather the fruit/ nut mixture into a ball and mash together with your hands.
4 - Divide the mixture into the number of bars you want to make.
5 - With damp hands flatten the mixture into a rectangle 3-4" tall rectangle, cover tightly with the plastic wrap, and apply a lot of pressure. Repeat with all remaining mixture sections.
6 - Allow the mixture to chill flat in the refrigerator for one hour to overnight.
7 - Label and enjoy!

Cherry Cobbler

1/2 Cup Almonds
1/2 Cup Cashews
1 Cup Medjool Dates, Pitted
1 Cup Dried Cherries
1 Tb Honey
Pinch of Sea Salt
1/2 tsp Vanilla

Directions:
1 - Place all of the ingredients into a food processor. Pulse several times to start breaking the larger pieces up.
2 - Process the mixture for 1-3 minutes until everything is broken down into tiny pieces and sticking together.
3 - Gather the fruit/ nut mixture into a ball and mash together with your hands.
4 - Divide the mixture into the number of bars you want to make.
5 - With damp hands flatten the mixture into a rectangle 3-4" tall rectangle, cover tightly with the plastic wrap, and apply a lot of pressure. Repeat with all remaining mixture sections.
6 - Allow the mixture to chill flat in the refrigerator for one hour to overnight.
7 - Label and enjoy!

Key Lime Pie

1/2 Cup Almonds
1/2 Cup Cashews
1 Cup Medjool Dates, Pitted
1 Cup Shredded Coconut
Zest & Juice 1 Lime
Pinch of Sea Salt
1/2 tsp Vanilla

Directions:

1 - Place all of the ingredients into a food processor. Pulse several times to start breaking the larger pieces up.

2 - Process the mixture for 1-3 minutes until everything is broken down into tiny pieces and sticking together.

3 - Gather the fruit/ nut mixture into a ball and mash together with your hands.

4 - Divide the mixture into the number of bars you want to make.

5 - With damp hands flatten the mixture into a rectangle 3-4" tall rectangle, cover tightly with the plastic wrap, and apply a lot of pressure. Repeat with all remaining mixture sections.

6 - Allow the mixture to chill flat in the refrigerator for one hour to overnight.

7 - Label and enjoy!

Coconut Cream Pie

1/2 Cup Almonds
1/2 Cup Cashews
1 Cup Medjool Dates, Pitted
1 Cup Shredded Coconut
2 Tb Coconut Oil
1/2 tsp Vanilla

Directions:
1 - Place all of the ingredients into a food processor. Pulse several times to start breaking the larger pieces up.
2 - Process the mixture for 1-3 minutes until everything is broken down into tiny pieces and sticking together.
3 - Gather the fruit/ nut mixture into a ball and mash together with your hands.
4 - Divide the mixture into the number of bars you want to make.
5 - With damp hands flatten the mixture into a rectangle 3-4" tall rectangle, cover tightly with the plastic wrap, and apply a lot of pressure. Repeat with all remaining mixture sections.
6 - Allow the mixture to chill flat in the refrigerator for one hour to overnight.
7 - Label and enjoy!.

Pumpkin Pie

1/2 Cup Almonds
1/2 Cup Pumpkin Seeds
1 Cup Medjool Dates, Pitted
1/4 tsp Ground Ginger
1/4 tsp Cinnamon
Pinch of Sea Salt
1/2 tsp Vanilla

Directions:
1 - Place all of the ingredients into a food processor. Pulse several times to start breaking the larger pieces up.
2 - Process the mixture for 1-3 minutes until everything is broken down into tiny pieces and sticking together.
3 - Gather the fruit/ nut mixture into a ball and mash together with your hands.
4 - Divide the mixture into the number of bars you want to make.
5 - With damp hands flatten the mixture into a rectangle 3-4" tall rectangle, cover tightly with the plastic wrap, and apply a lot of pressure. Repeat with all remaining mixture sections.
6 - Allow the mixture to chill flat in the refrigerator for one hour to overnight.
7 - Label and enjoy!

Cherry Pie

1 Cup Almonds
1 Cup Medjool Dates, Pitted
1 Cup Dried Cherries
Pinch of Sea Salt
1/2 tsp Vanilla

Directions:
1 - Place all of the ingredients into a food processor. Pulse several times to start breaking the larger pieces up.
2 - Process the mixture for 1-3 minutes until everything is broken down into tiny pieces and sticking together.
3 - Gather the fruit/ nut mixture into a ball and mash together with your hands.
4 - Divide the mixture into the number of bars you want to make.
5 - With damp hands flatten the mixture into a rectangle 3-4" tall rectangle, cover tightly with the plastic wrap, and apply a lot of pressure. Repeat with all remaining mixture sections.
6 - Allow the mixture to chill flat in the refrigerator for one hour to overnight.
7 - Label and enjoy!

Blueberry Pie

1 Cup Almonds
1 Cup Medjool Dates, Pitted
1 Cup Dried Blueberries
Pinch of Sea Salt
1/2 tsp Vanilla

Directions:
1 - Place all of the ingredients into a food processor. Pulse several times to start breaking the larger pieces up.
2 - Process the mixture for 1-3 minutes until everything is broken down into tiny pieces and sticking together.
3 - Gather the fruit/ nut mixture into a ball and mash together with your hands.
4 - Divide the mixture into the number of bars you want to make.
5 - With damp hands flatten the mixture into a rectangle 3-4" tall rectangle, cover tightly with the plastic wrap, and apply a lot of pressure. Repeat with all remaining mixture sections.
6 - Allow the mixture to chill flat in the refrigerator for one hour to overnight.
7 - Label and enjoy!

Pecan Pie

1/2 Cup Pecans
1/2 Cup Almonds
1 Cup Medjool Dates, Pitted
Pinch of Sea Salt
1/2 tsp Vanilla

Directions:
1 - Place all of the ingredients into a food processor. Pulse several times to start breaking the larger pieces up.
2 - Process the mixture for 1-3 minutes until everything is broken down into tiny pieces and sticking together.
3 - Gather the fruit/ nut mixture into a ball and mash together with your hands.
4 - Divide the mixture into the number of bars you want to make.
5 - With damp hands flatten the mixture into a rectangle 3-4" tall rectangle, cover tightly with the plastic wrap, and apply a lot of pressure. Repeat with all remaining mixture sections.
6 - Allow the mixture to chill flat in the refrigerator for one hour to overnight.
7 - Label and enjoy!

Apple Pie

1/2 Cup Almonds
1/2 Cup Walnuts
1 Cup Medjool Dates, Pitted
1 Cup Dried Apple
Pinch of Sea Salt
1 tsp Cinnamon

Directions:

1 - Place all of the ingredients into a food processor. Pulse several times to start breaking the larger pieces up.

2 - Process the mixture for 1-3 minutes until everything is broken down into tiny pieces and sticking together.

3 - Gather the fruit/ nut mixture into a ball and mash together with your hands.

4 - Divide the mixture into the number of bars you want to make.

5 - With damp hands flatten the mixture into a rectangle 3-4" tall rectangle, cover tightly with the plastic wrap, and apply a lot of pressure. Repeat with all remaining mixture sections.

6 - Allow the mixture to chill flat in the refrigerator for one hour to overnight.

7 - Label and enjoy!

PART 3
RESOURCES

BONUS RECIPES

Raw Homemade Granola

Yield:
Approx. 3 Cups

Ingredients:
1 Cup Soaked & Dehydrated Buckwheat
1/4 Cup Ground Flaxseeds
1/4 Cup Shredded Coconut
1/4 Cup Sunflower Seeds
1/4 Cup Cashew Halves or Pieces
1/4 Cup Raisins/ Gogi Berries/ Your Choice of Fruit
1 Tb Coconut or Flax Oil
1/3 Cup Pure Maple Syrup or Agave
1 Vanilla Bean Scraped

Directions:
1 - Mix all the dry ingredients in a large bowl.
2 - In a small bowl whisk the wet ingredients and the vanilla bean until combined.
3 - Pour the wet ingredients over the dry and mix thoroughly to coat all the dry ingredients.
4 - Spread out onto a thin layer on a dehydrator sheet covered with a non stick mat.
5 - Place in a dehydrator set at 114 for 10-12 hours, or until the granola is sticky but forming clumps that hold together.
6 - Place in an airtight container and store the granola in the freezer for longer shelf life and excellent crunch.

Raw Vanilla Liquid Extract

Yield:
1 Cup

Ingredients:
4 Whole Vanilla Beans
1 Cup Purified Water

Directions:
1 - Using a very sharp chef's knife, chop the beans into 1" pieces.
2- Combine the beans and water in a high speed blender. Set on high, blend until the mixture is chocolate brown and no pieces of the beans remain visible.
3 - Store the vanilla liquid in a sealed glass jar. It can be stored for up to 3 months in the refrigerator or freeze in ice cube trays for longer storage.
* Make a smoothie or almond milk before cleaning the blender to take advantage of the extra left over vanilla flavoring in the blender bucket.

ONLINE RESOURCES

Author's Website:
http://www.AuthorRachel.com

Book's Website:
http://www.RawEnergyBarInvasion.com

Energy Bar How To Demonstration
http://EnergyBarDemo.AuthorRachel.com

ABOUT THE AUTHOR

Rachel Frank is an Amazon Bestselling Author in Women's Health, Stress Management, and Special Diets. She was born in Rochester, NY and grew up in Western NY. She married an Active Duty Army Service Member and has moved across the United States to places like Hawaii and South Carolina. She is a PhD candidate in Health Psychology, has a Master of Science in Psychology from Walden University, and is a Board Certified Holistic Health Coach with the American Association of Drugless Practitioners. She writes, speaks, and teaches about holistic health, self help, healthy living, and healthy cooking. An avid animal lover, Rachel cares for 16 rescue animals and brings that nurturing and supportive spirit into her work.

Thank you for buying Raw Energy Bar Invasion!

If you loved this cookbook and have a moment to spare, I would really appreciate a short review on the page where you bought this book. Your help in spreading the word is greatly appreciated. Reviews make a world of difference in helping other readers find this book.

You can sign up to be notified of the future books, classes, and pre-release specials here:

http://www.AuthorRachel.com

Read Healthy Cookbooks

by Rachel Frank

Available now on Amazon

Take eCourses by Rachel Frank

Available Summer 2013 on UDemy

www.UDemy.com

Listen to Relaxation and Hypnosis Audios

by Rachel Frank

Available now on Amazon

RACHEL FRANK

6556494R00048

Made in the USA
San Bernardino, CA
11 December 2013